CODE FOR OBESITY : An essential guide to control and lose weight permanently & Stay healthy

Michael I. Roberts

Table of content

Chapter 1

WHY YOU ALWAYS WANT FOOD

14 Reasons Why You're Always Hungry

Hunger is your body's natural cue that it needs further food.

When you 're empty, your stomach may " growl " and feel empty, or you may get a headache, feel perverse, or be unfit to concentrate.

The utmost people can go several hours between reflections before feeling empty again, though this is n't the case for everyone.

There are several possible explanations for this, including a diet that lacks protein, fat, or fiber, as well as inordinate stress or dehumidification.

This composition discusses 14 reasons for inordinate hunger.

1. You 're not eating enough protein

Consuming enough protein is important for appetite control.

Protein has hunger- reducing parcels that may help you automatically consume smaller calories during the day. It works by adding the product of hormones that gesture wholeness and reducing the situations of hormones that stimulate hunger.

Due to these goods, you may feel empty constantly if you 're not eating enough protein.

In one study, 14 men with redundant weight who consumed 25% of their calories from protein for 12 weeks endured a 50% reduction in their desire for late-night snacking, compared with a group that consumed less protein.

Also, those with an advanced protein input reported lesser wholeness throughout the day and smaller compulsive studies about food.
numerous different foods are high in protein, so it's not delicate to get enough of it through your diet. Including a source of protein in every mess can help inordinate hunger.

Beast products, similar to meat, flesh, fish, and eggs, contain high quantities of protein.

This nutrient is also set up in some dairy products, including milk and yogurt, as well as many factory-grounded foods like legumes, nuts, seeds, and whole grains.

SUMMARY

Protein plays an important part in appetite control by regulating your hunger hormones. For this reason, you may feel empty constantly if you do n't eat enough of it.

2. You 're not sleeping enough

Getting acceptable sleep is extremely important for your health.

Sleep is needed for the proper functioning of your brain and vulnerable system, and getting enough of it's associated with a lower threat of several habitual ails, including heart complaints and cancer.

Also, sleeping enough is a factor in appetite control, as it helps regulate ghrelin, the appetite- stimulating hormone. Lack of sleep leads to advanced ghrelin situations, which is why you may feel peckish when you're sleep deprived.

In one study, 15 people who were sleep deprived for only 1 night reported being significantly more empty and chose 14 larger portion sizes, compared with a group that slept for 8 hours.

Getting enough sleep also helps insure acceptable situations of leptin, a hormone that promotes passions of wholeness.

To keep your hunger situations well managed, it’s generally recommended to get at least 8 hours of continued sleep each night.

SUMMARY
Sleep privation is known to beget oscillations in your hunger hormone situations and may leave you feeling empty more constantly.

3. You ’re eating too numerous refined carbs
Refined carbs have been largely reused and stripped of their fiber, vitamins, and minerals.

One of the most popular sources of refined carbs is white flour, which is set up in numerous grain- grounded foods like chuck and pasta. Foods like soda pop, delicacy, and ignited goods, which are made with reused sugars, are also considered to be ameliorated carbs.

Since ameliorated carbs warrant filling fiber, your body digests them veritably snappily. This is a major reason why you may be empty constantly if you eat a lot of refined carbs, as they don't promote significant passions of wholeness.

Likewise, eating refined carbs may lead to rapid-fire harpoons in your blood sugar. This leads to increased situations of insulin, a hormone responsible for transporting sugar into your cells.

When a lot of insulin is released formerly in response to high blood sugar, it snappily removes sugar from your blood, which may lead to an unforeseen drop in blood sugar situations, a condition known as hypoglycemia.

Low blood sugar situations tell your body that it needs further food, which is another reason why you may feel empty frequently if ameliorated carbs are a regular part of your diet.

To reduce your refined carb input, simply replace them with nutrient-rich, whole foods like vegetables, fruit, legumes, and whole grains. These foods are still high in carbs, but they're rich in fiber, which helps keep hunger well managed.

SUMMARY
Refined carbs warrant fiber and beget blood sugar oscillations, which are the primary reasons why eating too numerous of them may leave you feeling empty.

4. Your diet is low in fat
Fat plays a crucial part in keeping you full.

This is incompletely due to its slow gastrointestinal conveyance time, meaning that it takes longer for you to digest and remains in your stomach for a long period. Also, eating fat may lead to the release of colorful wholeness- promoting hormones.

For these reasons, you may feel frequent hunger if your diet is low in fat.

One study including 270 grown-ups with rotundity set up that those who followed a low fat diet had significant increases in jones
for carbs and preferences for high- sugar foods, compared with a group that consumed a low carb diet.

Likewise, those in the low fat group reported more passions of hunger than the group that followed a low carb eating pattern.

There are numerous nutrient- thick, high fat foods that you can include in your diet to increase your fat input. Certain types of fats, similar as medium- chain triglycerides(MCTs) and omega- 3 adipose acids, have been studied the most for their capability to reduce appetite.

The richest food source of MCT is coconut oil painting, while omega- 3 adipose acids are set up in adipose fish like salmon, tuna, and sardines. You can also get omega- 3s from factory- grounded foods, similar as walnuts and flaxseeds.

Other sources of nutrient-rich, high fat foods include avocados, olive oil painting, eggs, and full fat yogurt.

SUMMARY

You may feel empty frequently if you do n't eat enough fat. That's because fat plays a part in decelerating digestion and adding the product of wholeness-promoting hormones.

5. You 're not drinking enough water

Proper hydration is incredibly important for your overall health.

Drinking enough water has several health benefits, including promoting brain and heart health and optimizing exercise performance. Also, water keeps your skin and digestive system healthy.

Water is also relatively filling and has the implicit to reduce appetite when consumed before reflections.

In one study, 14 people who drank 2 mugs of water before a mess ate nearly 600 smaller calories than those who did n't drink any water.

Due to water's part in keeping you full, you may find that you feel empty constantly if you 're not drinking enough of it.

Passions of thirst can be incorrect for passions ofhunger.However, it may help to drink a glass or two of water to find out if you 're just thirsty, If you 're always empty.

To ensure you 're duly doused , simply drink water when you feel thirsty. Eating lots of water-rich foods, including fruits and vegetables, will also contribute to your hydration needs.

SUMMARY

You may always be empty if you 're not drinking enough water. That's because it has an appetite- reducing parcels. Also, you may be mistaking passions of thirst for passions of hunger.

6. Your diet lacks fiber

Still, you may feel empty constantly, If your diet lacks fiber.

Consuming lots of high fiber foods helps keep hunger well managed. High fiber foods decelerate your stomach's evacuating rate and take longer to digest than low fiber foods.

Also, a high fiber input influences the release of appetite- reducing hormones and the product of short-chain adipose acids, which have been shown to have wholeness- promoting goods.

It's important to note that there are different types of fiber, and some are better than others at keeping you full and precluding hunger. Several studies have set up that answerable fiber, or fiber that dissolves in water, is more filling than undoable fiber.

numerous different foods, similar as oatmeal, flaxseeds, sweet potatoes, oranges, and Brussels sprouts, are excellent sources of answerable fiber.

Not only does a high fiber diet help reduce hunger, but it's also associated with several other health benefits, similar to a reduced threat of heart complaint, diabetes, and rotundity.

To ensure you 're getting enough fiber, conclude for a diet that's rich in whole, factory- grounded foods, similar as fruits, vegetables, nuts, seeds, legumes, and whole grains.

SUMMARY

Still, you may find that you're always empty, If your diet lacks fiber. This is because fiber plays a part in reducing your appetite and keeping you full.

7. You eat while you 're distracted

Still, you may frequently eat while you're distracted, If you live a busy life.

Although it may save you time, distracted eating can be mischievous to your health. It's associated with lesser appetite, increased calorie input, and weight gain.

The primary reason for this is because distracted eating reduces your mindfulness of how important you 're consuming. It prevents you from getting your body's wholeness signals as efficiently as when you 're not detracted.

Several studies have shown that those who engage in distracted eating are peckish
than those who avoid distractions during mealtimes.

In one study, 88 women were instructed to eat either while distracted or sitting in silence. Those who were detracted were less full and had a significantly lesser desire to eat further throughout the day, compared with the non-distracted eaters.

Another study set up that people who distracted themselves with a computer game during lunch were less full than those who didn't play the game. Also, the distracted eaters consumed 48 further food in a test that passed later that day.

To avoid distracted eating, you can try rehearsing awareness, minimizing screen time, and silencing your electronic bias. This will allow you to sit down and taste your food, helping you better fete your body's wholeness signals.

SUMMARY
Deracted eating may be a reason why you're always empty, as it makes it delicate for you to fe feat your passions of wholeness.

8. You exercise a lot

individuals who exercise constantly burn a lot of calories.

This is especially true if you regularly share in high-intensity exercise or engage in physical exertion for long durations, similar as in marathon training.

Research has shown that those who exercise roundly on a regular basis tend to have a briskly metabolism, which means that they burn further calories at rest than those who exercise relatively or live sedentary cultures.

More Lately, still, a 2014 methodical review of 103 studies set up no harmonious substantiation to support increased energy input during exercise. fresh randomized studies are demanded.

In one study, 10 men who engaged in a vigorous 45-minute drill increased their overall metabolic rate by 37 for the day, compared with another day when they didn't exercise.

Another study set up that women who exercised at a high intensity every day for 16 days burned 33 further calories throughout the day than a group that didn't exercise and 15 further calories than moderate trampolinists. The results were analogous for men.

Although several studies have shown exercise to be salutary for suppressing appetite, there's some substantiation that vigorous, long- term trampolinists tend to have lesser favors than those who don't exercise.

You can help inordinate hunger from exercise simply by eating further to fuel your exercises. It's utmost helpful to increase your input of filling foods that are high in fiber, protein, and healthy fats.

Another result is to cut back on the time you spend exercising or reduce the intensity of your exercises.

It’s important to note that this substantially applies to those who are avaricious athletes and work out constantly at a high intensity or for long periods.However, you presumably do n’t need to increase your calorie input, If you exercise relatively.

SUMMARY

individuals who regularly exercise at a high intensity or for long durations tend to have lesser favors and brisk metabolisms. Therefore, they may witness frequent hunger.

9. You ’re drinking too important alcohol

Alcohol is well known for its appetite- stimulating goods.

Studies have shown that alcohol may inhibit hormones that reduce appetite, similar to leptin, especially when it's consumed before or with reflections. For this reason, you may feel empty frequently if you drink too much alcohol.

In one study, 12 men who drank1.5 ounces(40 mL) of alcohol before lunch ended up consuming 300 more calories at the mess than a group that drank only0.3 ounces(10 mL).

Also, those who drank further alcohol ate 10 further calories throughout the entire day, compared with the group that drank less. They were also more likely to consume high quantities of high fat and salty foods.

Another study set up that 26 people who drank 1 ounce(30 mL) of alcohol with a mess consumed 30 further calories, compared with a group that avoided alcohol.

Alcohol may not only make you peckish, but it also impairs the part of your brain that controls judgment and tone- control. This may lead you to eat more, anyhow of how empty you're.

To reduce hunger- converting goods of alcohol, it's stylish to consume it relatively or avoid it fully.

SUMMARY

Drinking too much alcohol may make you feel empty constantly due to its part in dwindling the product of hormones that promote wholeness.

10. You drink your calories

Liquid and solid foods affect your appetite in different ways.

Still, similar to smoothies, mess relief shakes, If you consume a lot of liquid foods.

One major reason for this is that liquids pass through your stomach more snappily than solid foods do.

Likewise, some studies suggest that liquid foods don't have as great of an impact on the repression of hunger-promoting hormones, compared with solid foods.

Eating liquid foods also tends to take less time than eating solid foods. This may lead you to want to eat more, only because your brain has n't had enough time to reuse wholeness signals.

In one study, people who consumed a liquid snack reported lower wholeness and further passions of hunger than those who consumed a solid snack. They also consumed 400 further calories throughout the day than the solid- snack group.

To help frequent hunger, it may help to concentrate on incorporating further solid, whole foods into your diet.

SUMMARY

Liquid foods don't have the same goods on keeping you full and satisfied as solid foods do. For this reason, you may feel empty constantly if liquids are a major part of your diet.

11. You 're exorbitantly stressed-out
Redundant stress is known to increase appetite.

This is substantially due to its goods on adding situations of cortisol, a hormone that has been shown to promote hunger and food jones. For this reason, you might find that you're always empty if you witness frequent stress.

In one study, 59 women who were exposed to stress consumed further calories throughout the day and ate significantly sweeter foods than women who weren't stressed.

Another study compared the eating habits of 350 youthful girls. Those with advanced stress situations were more likely to gormandize than those with lower situations of stress. The girls with high stress situations also reported advanced inputs of low- nutrient snacks like chips and eyefuls.

Numerous strategies can help you reduce your stress situations. Some options include exercise and deep breathing.

SUMMARY

Inordinate stress is a reason why you may be empty constantly, given its capability to increase cortisol situations in the body.

12. You're taking certain specifics

Several specifics may increase your appetite as a side effect.

The most common appetite- converting specifics include antipsychotics, similar to clozapine and olanzapine, as well as antidepressants, mood stabilizers, corticosteroids, and anti seizure medicines.

Also, some diabetes specifics, similar as insulin, insulin secretagogues, and thiazolidinediones, are known to increase your hunger and appetite.

There's also some anecdotal substantiation that birth control capsules have appetite- stimulating parcels, but this isn't supported by strong scientific exploration.

Still, it may help to talk with your croaker about other treatment options, If you suspect that specifics are the cause of your frequent hunger. There may be indispensable specifics that do n't make you empty.

SUMMARY

Certain specifics beget increased appetite as a side effect. In turn, they may beget you to witness frequent hunger.

13. You eat too fast

The rate at which you eat may play a part in how empty you are.

Several studies have shown that fast eaters have lesser favors and a tendency to gormandize at reflections, compared with slow eaters. They're also more likely to have rotundity or redundant weight.

In one study involving 30 women, fast eaters consumed 10 further calories at a mess and reported significantly lower wholeness, compared with slow eaters.

Another study compared the goods of eating rates in those with diabetes. Those who ate a mess sluggishly came full more snappily and reported lower hunger 30 twinkles after the mess, compared with fast eaters.

These goods are incomplete due to the lack of biting and reduced mindfulness that do when you eat too much presto, both of which are necessary to palliate passions of hunger.

Also, eating sluggishly and biting completely gives your body and brain further time to release anti-hunger hormones and convey wholeness signals.

These ways are a part of eating.

Still, it may help to eat more sluggishly, If you're constantly empty. You can do this by

taking a many deep breaths before reflections
putting your chopstick down between mouthfuls
adding the extent to which you bite your food.

SUMMARY
Eating too snappily does n't allow your body enough time to fete wholeness, which may promote inordinate hunger.

14. You have a medical condition
Frequent hunger may be a symptom of complaint.

First, frequent hunger is a classic sign of diabetes. It occurs as a result of extremely high blood sugar situations and is generally accompanied by other symptoms, including inordinate thirst, weight loss, and fatigue.

Hyperthyroidism, a condition characterized by an hyperactive thyroid, is also associated with increased hunger. This is because it causes a redundant product of thyroid hormones, which are known to promote appetite.

Hypoglycemia, or low blood sugar situations, may also increase your hunger situations. Your blood sugar situations may fall if you have n't eaten for a while, an effect that may be aggravated by a diet high in refined carbs and sugar.

Still, hypoglycemia is also associated with medical conditions, similar to type 2 diabetes, hyperthyroidism, and order failure, among others.

Also, inordinate hunger is frequently a symptom of many other conditions, similar as depression, anxiety, and premenstrual pattern.

Still, it's important to talk with your croaker to admit a proper opinion and bandy treatment options, If you suspect that you may have one of these conditions.

SUMMARY

Inordinate hunger is a symptom of many specific medical conditions, which should be ruled out if you're constantly empty.

The nethermost line

Inordinate hunger is a sign that your body needs further food.

It's frequently a result of imbalanced hunger hormones, which may do for a variety of reasons, including a shy diet and certain life habits.

You may feel empty constantly if your diet lacks protein, fiber, or fat, all of which promote wholeness and reduce appetite. Extreme hunger is also a sign of shy sleep and habitual stress.

Also, certain specifics and nails are known to beget frequent hunger.

Still, it may be salutary to assess your diet and life to determine if there are changes you can make to help you feel more full, If you feel empty frequently.

Your hunger could also be a sign that you aren't eating enough, which can be answered by simply adding your food input.

In case you 're eating too snappily or detracted at mealtimes, you can also exercise aware eating, which aims to minimize distractions, increase your focus, and decelerate your chewing to help you realize when you 're full.

Chapter 2

HOW TO CREATE A UNIQUE EATING PLAN

6 Steps to Creating a Customized Diet Plan for Weight Loss

Achieving meaningful and long- continuing weight loss requires a thoughtful eating plan. Your body needs the right balance of nutrition and calories for sustained energy through exercises and diurnal conditioning. Maintaining that balance is the key to losing fat and keeping it off over time.

A successful diet plan for weight loss combines the vitamins and minerals your body needs to make muscle and maintain energy in one accessible and succulent menu. Follow these way to design a diet plan for weight loss that's specifically structured to support your life, pretensions, and habits.

STEP ONE AVOID CALORIE COUNTING DIET PLANS

Typical diet plans set a diurnal calorie thing. Swillers are anticipated to keep their consumption within a certain range each day with reflections that contain all the vital nutrients their bodies need to thrive. Still, this foundational belief sets numerous swillers up for failure before they indeed begin. We recommend an extensively different approach to calorie counting.

Why is a diurnal count the wrong way to approach nutritive input?

Every food has a different calorie content. Unless you eat nearly the same thing every day, it gets delicate to keep track of how important you 're consuming without laborious shadowing.

From spending time out with musketeers to going on holiday, there are a number of times when swillers simply ca n't maintain a strict diurnal count without immolating enjoyment of social situations.

To short- circuit temptation, numerous diet plans call for a " cheat day " that allows the picker to eat whatever they want without counting the calories. It's possible to stick to a diurnal restrictive calorie count and still not lose weight due to overindulging one day a week.

Diurnal calorie counts tend to encourage undereating. Swillers try to stay under their limits to save sweet poverty. Over time, too numerous missed calories negatively impact weight loss sweats.

Rather than setting yourself a set number of calories per day, we recommend you develop a diet plan that covers your nutritive musts to maintain a healthy life. This approach is exceptionally helpful in a weight loss program as it helps with your energy situations, is less restrictive, and allows you the freedom to enjoy what you want but in temperance. Determining your nutritive requirements is different for every person grounded on their age, weight, exertion situations, and other medical requirements.

Setting these nutritive pretensions or guidelines gives you the inflexibility to eat a variety of different foods to reach your weight loss pretensions. These nutritive pretensions concentrate on your input situations of protein, carbs, fats, vitamins, and minerals. Keeping these crucial factors balanced for what your body needs is a more successful approach for weight loss than calories counting.

STEP TWO CALCULATE YOUR MACROS

Overeating is n't just about how important you eat. You also need to ensure that you 're giving your body what it needs to grow muscle, melt fat, and keep your energy high. Macronutrients are the introductory structure blocks your body uses to negotiate these tasks. These abecedarian nutrients also represent the bulk of your sweet input. The three main orders for macros are

Carbohydrates. Simple and complex sugar chains break down in the body to give energy for muscles.
Fats. redundant calories are stored in fat cells to give exigency energy when fast- burning carbs are n't available. Fat is an essential element in numerous hormonal and brain functions as well.
Proteins. These hustler macros give sustainable energy and material used to repair and grow apkins throughout the body.

Balancing these macronutrients gives you the stylish chance of erecting the body you want without feeling depressed or exhausted. The general rule of thumb suggests that you divide your calorie input into 35 healthy fat, 40 protein, and 25 carbohydrates. For a more individualized rate, use an online calculator to determine your stylish blend.

STEP THREE DISCOVERY FOODS THAT FIT

Once you know how important you need to eat, spend some time changing foods that fit into your new life. An effective diet plan for weight loss must include foods that you 'll actuallyeat.However, it's doubtful that you 'll stick to your plan, If you do n't enjoy what you 're eating.

Still, it's also important to put some effort into trying new menu options. numerous swillers come to weight loss programs because of a limited diet that's high in empty calories. Adding further nutritive options to your diurnal menu is an essential step to creating a long- term eating plan.

launch by making a list of the foods and constituents that you love the most. Once your diet begins, aim to add one or two new fruits, vegetables, or grain selections each week to your list. It's helpful to also include data on the macronutrient content of each item, as this will help you decide how important of each of these constituents you can enjoy in each mess.

STEP FOUR STOCK UP ON FASHIONS

Now that you know what you can eat, start collecting a variety of fashions that feature your listed foods. Pay attention to medication instructions. The way you cook your food has a big effect on macronutrient content.

A large form selection is important in your diet plan for weight loss because it keeps you from getting weary. Losing interest in diurnal menus is the main reason numerous swillers do n't reach their pretensions. Variety ensures that you 'll always look forward to your coming serving. An online form book is a great way to store your fashions.

With enough exploration, you can conform your form collection to fit your preferences. Are you a nut of sweetbreads and afters? Find low- calorie performances of your favorite baked goods. Are gravies a necessary part of your diurnal dining experience? Look for manual performances of your most constantly used seasonings. Does the idea of giving up fried foods make you nervous? Look for fashions that use your roaster to pretend the crunchiness you crave without the fresh fat content.

For those who live life on the- go, collect a list of your most visited caffs. Ask the staff for nutritive information on their menu particulars. Use that data to produce a list of selections that fit within your salutary budget.

STEP FIVE SET AN EATING SCHEDULE

When you eat is just as important as what you eat. Our bodies go through cycles each day that affect our capability to metabolize stomach contents. Also, medical conditions or differences in body functions can change the way you reuse reflections.

For many, a diet plan for weight loss that follows the traditional 3 reflections a day paradigm does n't work. This is especially true for those who are aggressively cutting back their diurnal calorie input. Try to distance your reflections and snacks roughly 3 hours piecemeal. This keeps you from getting too empty and running for unhealthy options to fill your belly. Then are some other guidelines to help you make the perfect diet plan for weight loss.

Eat a stuffing regale to avoid late night snacking. Consume a high- protein breakfast within an hour of waking up. Stick to your listed mess plan. Still, see your croaker for help erecting a schedule that helps maintain the proper blood sugar situations, If you have diabetes or other glucose conditions that are impacted by your eating habits.

STEP SIX TRACK, DISSECT, AND ACCLIMATE

Use a food journal to keep track of your mess plan. This creates a record that allows you to readdress your eating habits and dissect the effectiveness of your plan. Make adaptations when demanded to keep yourself on track to your thin weight. Do n't be hysterical to change effects up if a certain salutary plan is n't furnishing the asked results.

VOLUNTARY STEP FIND A PROFESSIONAL DIET PLAN FOR WEIGHT LOSS

Luckily, you do n't have to struggle through weight loss alone. Med- Fit can help you develop a medically accurate diet plan for weight loss that helps you reach your target weight in a healthy way. communicate with us to get started on your customized weight loss trip moment.

HOW TO MEAL PLAN FOR WEIGHT LOSS

Mess planning can be a helpful tool if you ’re trying to lose weight.

When done right, it can help you produce the calorie deficiency needed for weight loss while furnishing your body with the nutritional foods it needs to serve and remain healthy.

Planning your reflections ahead can also simplify the mess fix process and save you time.

This composition explores the most important aspects of mess planning for weight loss, including many easy fashions and redundant tips to help you reach your pretensions.

How to mess plan for weight loss
When it comes to weight loss mess plans, the magnitude of options can be inviting. Then there are many effects to keep in mind when you search for the most suitable plan.

Creating a calorie deficiency in a nutrient- thick way
All weight loss plans have one thing in common — they get you to eat smaller calories than you burn.

Still, though a calorie deficiency will help you lose weight anyhow of how it’s created, what you eat is just as important as how important you eat. That's because the food choices you make are necessary in helping you meet your nutrient needs.

A good weight loss mess plan should follow some universal criteria

Includes plenitude of protein and fiber. Protein- and fiber-rich foods help keep you fuller for longer, reducing jones and helping you feel satisfied with lower portions.

Limits reused foods and added sugar. Rich in calories yet low in nutrients, these foods fail to stimulate wholeness centers in your brain and make it delicate to lose weight or meet your nutrient needs.

Includes a variety of fruits and vegetables. Both are rich in water and fiber, contributing to passions of wholeness. These nutrient-rich foods also make it easier to meet your diurnal nutrient conditions.

structure nutrient- thick reflections
To incorporate these tips into your weight loss mess plan, start by filling one- third to one- half of your plate with non-starchy vegetables. These are low in calories and give water, fiber, and numerous of the vitamins and minerals you need.

Also, fill one- quarter to one- third of your plate with protein-rich foods, similar as meat, fish, tofu, seitan, or legumes, and the remainder with whole grains, fruit, or stiff vegetables. These add protein, vitamins, minerals, and further fiber.

You can boost the flavor of your mess with a gusto of healthy fats from foods like avocados, olives, nuts, and seeds.

Some people may profit from having a snack to drift their hunger over between reflections. Protein- and fiber-rich snacks feel the most effective for weight loss.

Good exemplifications include apple slices with peanut adulation, vegetables and hummus, roasted chickpeas, or Greek yogurt with fruit and nuts.

SUMMARY
A successful weight loss mess plan should produce a calorie deficiency while meeting your nutrient needs.

Helpful tips to make mess planning work for you
An important aspect of a successful weight loss mess plan is its capability to help you keep the misplaced weight out.

Then are some tips to help increase your mess plan's long- term sustainability.

Pick a mess planning system that fits your routine
There are colorful ways to mess up plans, so be sure to pick the system that fits your routine.

You may decide to batch cook all of your reflections over the weekend, so you can fluently snare individual portions throughout the week. Alternately, you may prefer to cook daily, in which case, concluding to fix all of your constituents ahead of time might work stylish for you.

Still, you may conclude for a system that requires you to fill your refrigerator and closet with specific portions of foods each week while allowing you to extemporize when putting them together for reflections, If you do n't like following fashions or prefer a little further inflexibility.

Batch- shopping for groceries is another great strategy that helps save time while keeping your refrigerator and closet filled with nutrient- thick foods.

Consider trying an app

Apps can be a helpful tool in your mess planning magazine.

Some apps offer mess plan templates that you can alter grounded on your food preferences or disinclination. They can also be a handy way to keep track of your favorite fashions and save all of your data in one place.

What's more, numerous apps give customized grocery lists based on your named fashions or what's left over in your fridge, helping you save time and reduce food waste.

Pick enough fashions

Picking an acceptable number of fashions ensures that you have enough variety without taking you to spend all of your free time in the kitchen.

When opting how numerous rejections to make, look at your timetable to determine the number of times you ’re likely to eat out — whether for a date, customer regale, or brunch with musketeers.

Divide the remaining number of breakfasts, lunches, and feasts by the number of reflections that you can really cook or prepare for that week. This helps you determine the portions of each mess you ’ll need to fix.

Also, simply sift through your cookbooks or online food blogs to pick your fashions.

Consider snacks

Allowing yourself to get exorbitantly empty between reflections may push you to gormandize at your coming mess, making it more delicate to reach your weight loss pretensions.

Snacks can help lower hunger, promote passions of wholeness, and reduce the overall number of calories you eat per day.

Protein- and fiber-rich combinations, similar as nuts, roasted chickpeas, or veggies and hummus, appear stylish and suited to promote weight loss.

Still, keep in mind that some people tend to gain weight when adding snacks to their menu. So make sure you cover your results when applying this strategy.

insure variety

Eating a variety of foods is necessary in furnishing your body with the nutrients it needs.

That's why it's stylish to avoid mess plans that suggest batch cuisine 1 – 2 fashions for the whole week. This lack of variety can make it delicate to meet your diurnal nutrient requirements and lead to tedium over time, reducing your mess plan's sustainability.

Rather, ensure that your menu includes a variety of foods each day.

Speed up your mess fix time

mess preparing does n't have to mean long hours in the kitchen. Then there are many ways to speed up your mess fix time.

Stick to a routine. Picking specific times to plan the week's reflections, grocery shop, and cook can simplify your decision- making process and make your mess preparation process more effective.

Grocery shop with a list. Detailed grocery lists can reduce your shopping time. Try organizing your list by supermarket departments to help double back to a preliminarily visited section.

Pick compatible fashions. When batch cuisine, choose fashions that use different appliances. For case, one form may bear the roaster, no further than two burners on the stovetop, and no heating at all.

Record your chef times. Organize your workflow by starting with the form taking the longest cuisine time, also concentrate on the rest. Electric pressure cookers or slow cookers can further reduce cuisine times.
Inexperienced culinarians or those simply wanting to reduce the time spent in the kitchen may want to pick fashions that can be prepared in 15 – 20 twinkles from launch to finish.

Store and overheat your reflections safely
Storing and reheating your reflections safely can help save their flavor and minimize your threat of food poisoning.

Then are some government- approved food safety guidelines to keep in mind(16, 17)

Cook food completely. the utmost flesh should reach an internal temperature of at least 165 °F(75 °C) while cooking, as this kills most bacteria.

Thaw food in the refrigerator. Deliquescing firmed foods or reflections on your countertop can encourage bacteria to multiply.However, submerge foods in cold water, changing the water every 30 twinkles, If you 're short on time.

Reheat food safely. Make sure to overheat your reflections to at least 165 °F(75 °C) before eating. Frozen reflections should be eaten within 24 hours of defrosting.

Dispose of old food. Refrigerated reflections should be eaten within 3 – 4 days of being made, and frozen reflections should be consumed within 3 – 6 months.

SUMMARY

Picking a mess- planning system that works for you, along with an acceptable number and variety of reflections and snacks that can be cooked or reheated snappily and safely, increases your liability of sustainable weight loss.

Easy form ideas

Weight loss fashions do n't have to be exorbitantly complicated. Then are many easy- to- prepare ideas that bear a minimum number of constituents.

Mists. mists can be batch- cooked and firmed in individual portions. Be sure to include a lot of vegetables, as well as meat, seafood, sap, peas, or lentils. Add brown rice, quinoa, or potatoes if asked .

Manual pizza. Start your pizza with a veggie- or whole-grain grounded crust, thin subcaste of sauce, source of protein, similar as tempeh or lemon bone, and veggies. Top with a little rubbish and fresh leafy flora.

Salads. Salads are quick and protean. Start with lush flora, many various vegetables, and a source of protein. Top with olive oil painting and ginger and add nuts, seeds, whole grains, or stiff vegetables.

Pasta. Start with a whole- grain pasta of your choice and source of protein, similar to funk, fish, or tofu. Also mix in a tomato- ground pasta sauce or pesto and some vegetables like broccoli or spinach.

Slow cooker or electric pressure cooker fashions. These are great for making chili, masses, spaghetti sauce, and stew. Simply place your constituents in your device, start it, and let it do all the work for you.

Grain coliseums. Batch chef grains like quinoa or brown rice also top with your choice of protein, similar to funk or hard- boiled eggs,non-starchy veggies, and a healthy dressing of your relish.

SUMMARY

The form ideas are simple and bear veritably little time to make. They can also be prepared in a variety of ways, making them incredibly protean.

7- day menu

This sample menu includes a variety of nutrient-, fiber-, and protein-rich reflections to help you reach your weight loss pretensions.

Portions should be acclimated to your individual requirements. Snack exemplifications are included in this plan but remain fully voluntary.

Monday

Breakfast overnight oats made with rolled oats, chia seeds, and milk, outgunned with fresh berries and pumpkin seeds.

Lunch premade egg- and- veggie muffins with a fresh basil- and- tomato salad and some avocado

Snack mango- spinach smoothie

regale manual cauliflower- crust pizza outgunned with pesto, mushrooms, peppers, a sprinkle of spinach, and marinated funk or tempeh.

Tuesday

Breakfast breakfast smoothie made with kale, firmed cherries, banana, protein greasepaint, flax seeds, and milk

Lunch mixed green salad with cucumber, bell pepper, tomato, sludge, sweet potato, olives, and grilled salmon or roasted chickpeas

Snack sliced apple with peanut adulation

regale red lentil dahl served on a bed of baby spinach and brown rice

Wednesday
Breakfast Spanish omelet made with eggs, potatoes, onions, and peppers, served with a side of salsa
Lunch leftover red lentil dahl and fresh spinach over brown rice.

Snack manual trail blend using your favorite unsalted, unroasted nuts and thin dried fruit
regale funk or tofu meatballs in a marinara sauce served with spaghetti squash on a bed of mixed baby flora and outgunned with Parmesan rubbish or nutritive incentive.

Thursday
Breakfast yogurt outgunned with fresh fruit and diced walnuts.
Lunch kale salad is outgunned with a coddled egg or marinated seitan, as well as dried cranberries, cherry tomatoes, whole- grain pita chips, and an avocado-mango dressing.

Snack carrots, radishes, and cherry tomatoes dipped in hummus
regal beef or black- bean burger outgunned with lettuce, tomato, roasted peppers, caramelized onions, and pickles, served on a small whole- wheat bun and peppers and onions on the side.

Friday
Breakfast breakfast salad made with spinach, manual granola, walnuts, blueberries, coconut flakes, and a jeer

vinaigrette, as well as 1 – 2 hard- boiled eggs for redundant protein if you like.

Lunch manual veggie spring rolls, dipped in peanut adulation sauce and served with a side of raw veggies

Snack whole- wheat crackers with rubbish or a racy mashed black bean spread

regale chili served on a bed of flora and wild rice.

Saturday

Breakfast pumpkin flapjacks outgunned with Greek or factory- grounded yogurt, diced nuts, and fresh strawberries

Lunch leftover chili served on a bed of flora and wild rice

Snack nut- and- dried- fruit trail blend

regale shrimp or bean fajitas with grilled onions, bell peppers, and guacamole, served on a sludge tortilla.

Sunday

Breakfast overnight oats outgunned with diced pecans, mango, and coconut flakes

Lunch tuna or chickpea salad, served atop mixed flora with sliced avocado, sliced apple, and walnuts

Snack yogurt with fruit

regale grilled salmon or tempeh, potatoes, and sautéed kale

Ideas for salutary restrictions

Generally speaking, meat, fish, eggs, and dairy can be replaced by factory- grounded druthers

, similar to tofu, tempeh, seitan, sap, flax or chia seeds, as well as factory- ground milk and yogurts.

Gluten- containing grains and flours can be substituted for quinoa, millet, oats, buckwheat, amaranth, teff, sludge, and sludge.

Carb-rich grains and stiff vegetables can be replaced by lower- carb druthers.

For example, try spiralized polos or spaghetti squash rather than pasta, cauliflower rice rather than couscous or rice, lettuce leaves rather than taco shells, and seaweed or rice paper rather than tortilla wraps.

Just keep in mind that fully banning a food group may cause you to take supplements to meet your diurnal nutrient requirements.

SUMMARY

Weight loss reflections should be nutrient- thick and rich in protein and fiber. This mess plan can be acclimated for a variety of salutary restrictions but may bear you to take supplements if fully banning a food order.

The nethermost line

A good weight loss mess plan creates a calorie deficiency while furnishing all the nutrients you need.

Done right, it can be incredibly simple and save you a lot of time.

Picking a system that works for you can also reduce your liability of recovering weight.

All- in- all, mess planning is an incredibly useful weight loss strategy.

Chapter 3

HOW TO SOLVE WEIGHT LOSS CHALLENGES

6 Common Weight-Loss Challenges and How to Solve Them

The rearmost exploration is clear. There's no similar thing as a one- size- fits- all approach to weight loss. Who you're is the topmost variable if you 're trying to exfoliate pounds, and there are innumerous factors that will make it easier or harder for you — poor diet, lack of exercise, genetics, specifics and other life and environmental factors can all play a part.

Specific physiological circumstances, still, inflate the significance of certain approaches to weight loss. For that reason, fastening your sweats on what will give you the most bang for your buck is crucial. As with utmost effects, once you get some traction and the pounds begin to fall off, taking on fresh strategies can lead to fresh weight loss. There's a quick companion on weight-loss strategies to fit some common life challenges. Maybe at least one of these applies to you.

The Challenge People gain weight for different reasons as they progress. Chief among them is a decline in physical exertion. When you move less, a lesser number of calories get stored in the body as fat, rather than getting converted into energy to fuel exertion. What's more, we naturally lose muscle mass as we progress — overhead of 3- 5 after age 30 if you 're inactive — which, in turn, leads to a slower metabolism.

Strength training can help put the thickets on the loss of muscle mass, as well as make new muscle. Since muscle cells are far more metabolically active than fat cells, they burn further calories. As you increase your muscle mass, you also boost your metabolism.

Be sure to warm up before training, and start slowly to make strength without injuring yourself. Begin with two sessions a week of 10 reps of 8 – 10 different exercises for the upper and lower body and the core. use your own body weight for effects like pushups and pullups and 5- to 10- pound dumbbells for other exercises. You should feel like you ca n't do further than a redundant rep or two at the end of each exercise — if you can, it's time to increase the weight.

The Challenge slipping baby weight when you 're sleep-deprived and overwhelmed by an infant is maybe one of the biggest challenges of new fatherhood. Recommendations for weight gain among women who are of average weight hovers between 25 – 35 pounds, but numerous gain more. While utmost lose around 10 – 15 pounds in the first week after delivery, the rest can be slow to go.

The result: Good nutrition and a healthy amount of physical exertion(once you 're recovered) is important for new mothers for a number of reasons, especially if you 're bone- feeding. In the morning, light aerobic exertion is a great way to boost your mood and begin the process of slipping that redundant weight you gained(make sure you have the go- ahead from your croaker).

What's more, you can bring the baby along, so it doubles as a clinging exertion. When you have the go-ahead from your croaker, start with 1 – 2 long hauls of stroller walks. The Centers for Disease Control and Prevention estimates that just 30 twinkles of walking at4.5 long hauls per hour becks around 230 calories for a 154- pound person.

The Challenge People with a lower rudimentary metabolism can eat the exact same diet but burn smaller calories than someone with a normal metabolism. Worse yet, the fatigue that comes on with a slow metabolism makes exercise the last thing you want to do.

The Solution If you suspect you may have a below-average metabolism, getting your thyroid checked is essential. For those diagnosed with hypothyroidism, the proper combination of specifics can make a big difference in aiding with increased exertion and weight loss. As far as the stylish exercise authority, while it may be hard at first, exploration suggests that high- intensity interval training has the implicit ability to boost metabolism. This type of drill involves short bouts of all-eschewal trouble followed by ages of rest. The American College of Sports Medicine suggests doing 3 – 5 bouts of 30-alternate sprints followed by 4 –4.5-twinkles of rest in between each 3 times per week(be sure to include a prologue and cooldown).

The Challenge Hypoglycemia(aka low blood sugar) can beget weakness, headaches and fatigue. These effects make it especially tough to be physically active, which frequently contributes to weight gain and the incapability to exfoliate redundant pounds. Fortunately, the same salutary changes that can make a big difference in terms of regulating blood sugar also contribute to weight loss.

The result: Staying down from too important sugar and fat will help regulate your blood sugar situations, while contemporaneously forcing you to cut out some of the loftiest- calorie junk foods. Work on taking in further low-glycemic indicator complex carbohydrates, foods high in answerable fiber and healthy protein, like sword- cut oats, whole- grain pasta, nuts, fish, apples and eggplant.

The Challenge Not only do you not burn calories as efficiently as you formerly did, your metabolism also slows with age. This means numerous people pack on the pounds once they hit middle age, indeed those who have preliminarily norway prodded with weight.

The Solution Research published in the Journal of American Medical Association set up that middle- age women had to log a normal of 60 twinkles of moderate-intensity exercise to maintain weight over the long haul. While this is twice the typical tradition of 30 twinkles a day, other exploration supports the significance of aerobic training for middle- age grown-ups for weight loss and overall health. This could include walking, jogging, swimming, cycling and time spent on the elliptical.

The Challenge When hormones like cortisol, testosterone and leptin are n't performing the way they should, everything from your appetite to your energy situations can be affected. This can make it feel insolvable to slim down.

The Solution

While experts are still working on how to address this issue, life and salutary changes go a long way toward balancing your hormones, which can boost energy and help control jones. Start by logging your nutritive input in the MyFitnessPal app to determine if you 're getting the right balance of nutrients. Make nutritive adaptations depending on your particular situation, which can help pinpoint the root of the problem.

Sleep is another aspect of your diurnal life that requires your attention. exploration shows that when you do n't get enough of it, you crave more high- fat and high-carbohydrate foods. Getting an acceptable quantum of rest will help balance out the situations of leptin in your blood to check those jones.

1. Do n't skip breakfast, and get at least 10 grams of protein

Eating a balanced breakfast including protein, fat and carbs — will give you the energy you need for the day.

still, you 're starting the day on a dead battery, " says Ms, " If you skip breakfast. Kirkpatrick. " Studies show that advanced input of protein in the morning is also essential for squashing jones
later in the day. "

Good sources of protein include eggs, factory-grounded protein maquillages, picked toast with natural peanut adulation, and plain thin yogurt with berries and hemp seeds.

Skipping reflections can make your body suppose it's in starvation mode. " Think of Sumo wrestlers. They eat little or nothing all day, also eat a big mess late in the day — therefore their size and high fat- to- muscle rate, " she says.

2. Eat small reflections, or consider dieting

Take your pick of three reflections a day with two or three snacks, five or six small reflections a day, or eat every three to four hours.

Each of these approaches will keep your metabolism indeed and your blood sugar situations stable.

Balance will help your body function at its stylish and will help you avoid weight gain. " You do n't want your blood sugar to rise and fall as if you 're on a comber coaster. That will make your energy situations change and all your body processes work less efficiently, "Ms. Kirkpatrick says.

" It's better to have blood sugar situations that mimic a kiddo comber coaster. It may feel less instigative, but it wo n't throw off your metabolism as much. "

Another option to consider is fasting, she notes. Studies show that people who cleave to either an intermittent-fasting or time- confined feeding approach have a dropped threat of complaint, lower mortality and further success in losing weight.

3. Exercise relatively, and add some weights

A violent drill authority is great if you 're happy with your weight and are in good health. But if you 're floundering to exfoliate pounds, a moderate exercise program will work better for you.

Walking 30 twinkles on a regular basis will benefit you further than a violent 90- nanosecond routine you ca n't maintain.

" Moderate exercise is especially important if you have problems with blood sugar. A violent drill will add further stress to your body by making your blood sugar shaft and also fall, " saysMs. Kirkpatrick.

She adds that setting pretensions too high and failing to meet them will keep you from feeling successful. " It's better to set small pretensions and surpass them. "

Also, adding in at least three days of resistance training will help you increase muscle, speed up your metabolism and make weight loss easier.

4. Eat until you 're no longer empty, not until you 're full
When you feel full, it means you have over-fueled. " Stop giving your body calories it doesn't need, " saysMs. Kirkpatrick. " rather, hear to your hunger, and eat only when empty. "

The quantity of carbs, protein and healthy fat you need depends on lots of factors, including your weight loss pretensions, complaint status,etc.

Another tactic is to start big(at breakfast) and end small, tapering off your portion sizes as the day goes on.

5. Be cautious of emotional eating. '

When you eat because you 're stressed out or starved for comfort, mindfulness is half the battle. " numerous people get frustrated because they 've joined a fitness or a weight loss program, have done everything right, and just ca n't feel to lose weight, " saysMs. Kirkpatrick.

You may want to consider using hypnotism, contemplation or holistic psychotherapy to help you let go of old eating patterns, similar as eating for comfort rather than out of real hunger.

" People realize, ' wow, I eat when I 'm not that empty, ' or ' I flash back how apple pie at grandma's would console me when I was little. That's what I suppose when I crave a comfort moment, '" saysMs. Kirkpatrick.

After letting go of eating patterns that no longer serve you, you 'll find yourself fitting into clothes you have n't been suitable for at times.

Chapter 4

HOW TO KEEP OFF WEIGHT PERMANENTLY

20 Secrets to Permanent Weight Loss

Do- overs are what your parents use to give you when you missed an easy hole on the mini-golf course. But sorely, with majority, comes" grown- up" liabilities, leaving little to no time for alternate shots especially when it comes to your long- term happy weight. Slipping pounds takes innumerous hours of fidelity, so if you've formerly gone through the grind to reach your thin weight, do you really want to do it again? We did not suppose so. You presumably want endless weight loss.

So, go ahead and stroke yourself on the reverse for all that you've fulfilled. But while you are at it, why not start allowing about how you are going to maintain your new body for the long haul? To help make it possible, we have come with easy ways for how to lose weight and keep it off permanently!

Pick many endless weight loss tips from the list below, stick to'em like it's your job, and prepare to stay in your skinny jeans for life. And for some redundant provocation, why not check out these 15 Uncredited Weight Loss Tips That Actually Work?

1 Do not do style diets

Within two times of overeating, between 18 and 30 percent of swillers can recapture over half the weight they lost, according to exploration presented at ENDO 2016, the periodic meeting of the Endocrine Society. The reason? They all slimmed down with the help of a diet, which by description is short term and does not produce life long results. To hit your thin weight and stay there, you need to make endless changes to your life. Not sure how? Check out these healthy eating habits for some alleviation.

2 Strength train

While it's possible to lose weight without doing a single pushup or burpee, in order to keep it off permanently, physical exertion is must, says JamesO. Hill, PhD,co-founder of the National Weight Control Registry a 25- time ongoing, prospective disquisition of long-term successful weight loss conservation.

But not all exercises are created equal. Although cardio gets all of the glory, interval and strength training are the real icons in the world of weight conservation. These styles of exercise will help you replace flab with hard, sexy muscle which will boost your metabolism and make it easier to keep off those sneaky pounds.

For the stylish results, do strength or interval training twice a week and aim for an hour of physical exertion a day — that could mean walking, swimming or running errands. Just get off your tush and move! Why an hour? The maturity of successful disasters(90 percent!) who have maintained their weight loss for a normal of5.5 times report moving for about an hour a day, according to the National Weight Control Registry.

3 Walk when you can

To insure you fit in those 60 twinkles and fit in further diurnal way, reevaluate your commute. On the days that I've to skip the spa, I force myself to walk home from work rather of hopping in a hack or taking the bus.However, cycle to the office once a week or situate your auto further down from the entrance, If you drive to work. still you decide to do it, the further way you take, the better. The maturity of people(52 percent) who have lost weight and kept it off report walking for an hour a day, according to an rotundity study. So, fit in those way wherever you can! And to get further out of each and every stride, check out these tips for walking for weight loss!

4 Only eat if you are empty — not wearied

Constantly eating when you do not need the energy is a major contributor to weight gain. Before you pop a commodity into your mouth, ask yourself why you are eating.(We are looking at youMs. Office Candy Bowl.) Are you actually empty or are you just angry, stressed, anxious, or weary? If it's any of the ultimate passions, healthy snacks like carrot sticks and apples will not feel appealing.However, oath to not eat anything at each, If you are not empty enough to eat at a factory.

5 Weigh yourself

Recent Cornell University findings suggest that flinching down from the scale can beget those former pounds to skulk back onto your frame not what you want! According to elderly author David Levitsky, people who weigh themselves daily and track the results are more likely to lose weight and keep it off than those who check in less frequently. The system" forces you to be apprehensive of the connection between your eating and your weight," Levitsky said in a press statement." The scale also acts as a priming medium, making you conscious of food and enabling you to make choices that are harmonious with your weight." For indeed further ways to shrink your gut, check out these stylish weight loss tips.

6 Exercise in the morning

We formerly told you that sticking to a fitness routine is an absolute must-have for weight conservation but that does not make changing the time — or provocation — after a busy workday any easier. The result of the problem: Wake up an hour and a half beforehand and fit in your drill before heading to the office. If you are over at 5a.m. with nothing else to do but break a sweat, odds are low enough that you will skip out on your charge camp or spin class. For further creative ways to stay motivated in the morning, check out these delightful ways to lose weight.

7 Put your exercises on your schedule

Can not bear the study of rising before the sun? At the morning of each week, take out a diary and schedule all of your exercises for the days ahead.However, odds are far lower you will fit in your fitness, If you just let your week and unfold aimlessly. record an appointment with a coach or a friend, book a class, or fit it in at home.

8 Meal fix

Your exercises are not the only effects you need to plan ahead to stay fit for life, you will also need to collude out your reflections." People have a much better chance of having a slim midriff if they plan when they're going to eat and what they're going to eat," says Mark Langowski, celebrity coach and author of Body By Mark Wellness." Before I go to bed, I look at my schedule for the coming day and plan out what I'm going to eat and where I'll eatit.However, it'll be 3 p, If you let the day begin without planning.me. before you know it and you will wind up making an unhealthy decision."

9 Store healthy reflections in the freezer

Registered dietitian and Fellow of the American Academy of Nutrition and Dietetics, ChristineM. Palumbo, RD agrees but takes a slightly different approach: mess fix" Identity three reflections you can prepare with closet masses and start cooking. Store the reflections in your freezer so you always have healthy commodities on hand when hunger strikes. For illustration, my go- to reflections include risotto with frozen shrimp and asparagus, vegetable barley, and red lentil haze. Your thing should be to replace the reflections whenever your store starts running low.``

10 Find a probative fitness group

How important your close musketeers weigh, plays a major part in how much you will weigh, say Harvard School of Public Health experimenters. In fact, their findings suggest that a person's chance of getting fat increases by 57% if a close friend is fat and it makes sense If your musketeers all love meeting up for burgers and beers on the regulation, it'll be really hard to stay on track with your healthy life. Our advice? From time to time suggest getting into other types of conditioning like yoga or a healthy cuisine class. You could also consider hosting get- togethers at your house so you can control the menu.

Another tip: Try to meet new people who enjoy living the healthy life you now lead.(A spa class or hiking group is a great place to introduce yourself!) This will help add a healthy balance to your life, without remonstrating your long- time besties to the check. For further ways to maintain your newfound flat abs, check out these stylish foods for muscle description!

11 Eat frequently

Eating constantly might sound counterintuitive if you are trying to keep the pounds out, but munching constantly throughout the day is crucial to blood sugar and hunger operation, explains registered dietitian Isabel Smith, MS, RD, CDN. When you eat commodity every three or four hours, it keeps your metabolism humming and you will noway get too empty. This ensures you will always be in a position to make smart diet opinions which is crucial to keeping the weight out long term. Not sure what to eat between reflections? Check out these 50- calorie snacks!

12 Hold the extras

Despite conventional wisdom, maintaining a major weight loss does not mean giving up croissants and eyefuls for good. It does, still, bear cutting calories where you will not miss em anyway so indulging from time to time will not do any damage to your midriff. exchange feasts for apple slices at McDonald's, keep the rubbish off your sandwiches and salads and ask for the sauce on the side when you dine out at an eatery. Believe it or not, these simple tweaks will save you hundreds of calories — without drastically altering the taste of your reflections. For indeed further calorie-saving tips, check out these ways to cut calories!

13 Eat breakfast diurnal

78 percent of National Weight Control Registry members who have lost a normal of 66 lbs and kept it off for5.5 times — regularly eat breakfast, according to a report published in rotundity. Though experimenters have not discovered a definite connection between the morning mess and weight loss, one proposition is that when you start your day with healthy food and eating it helps set a healthy tone for the rest of the day. To get on board, scourge up one of these late oats fashions or enjoy an omelet with some Ezekiel chuck
and some berries.

14 Keep triggers down

Nearly everyone has heard the rule that it's okay to eat anything and everything so long as you do so in temperance — but that may not be the stylish approach to lifelong weight conservation, according to 2015 PLOS ONE findings. The study of814 people stated that the maturity of the time, varied diets lead to weight gain.

" Though it can be scary to imagine fully cutting out the foods that you love, eating everything in moderation is actually near insolvable — especially when it comes to foods with addictive parcels, like sugar. You will probably find yourself going back further and further which can decelerate your weight loss results," explains registered dietitian Cassie Bjork,RD." That is why it's actually more salutary to fully cut out the foods that increase your jones

and keep you wanting further." For illustration, if you know that chocolate is your# 1 detector food it's stylish to cut it out altogether rather than trying to stick to a small serving. In the mood for commodity sweets? Check out these succulent weight loss smoothies!

15 Limit yourself to three

Fun fact National Weight Control Registry members, who have all lost 30 pounds or further and kept it off for at least a time, eat2.5 reflections per week at a eatery — and only 0.74 reflections per week at presto- food caffs like Burger King and McDonald's — according to an American Journal of Clinical Nutrition report. And we've to say, it's a smart move. Limiting the number of times you dine down from home is an easy way to keep redundant calories, swab, sugar, and fat off of your plate without a second of study. Dine out no further than three times per week — and stick to these low- calorie eatery reflections under 500 calories — to keep your midriff trim and spare!

16 Focus on flavonoids

Sure, all fruits and veggies are healthy and low- cal, but did you know that when it comes to keeping down those midriff- expanding pounds, flavonoid-rich foods like bananas, strawberries, grapes, pears, onions, peppers, and celery are the stylish bets? In a 2016 British Medical Journal study of,000 middle-aged and aged people, those who ate a diet rich in flavonoid- filled foods maintained their weight better than those who didn't — and it makes a lot of sense. before findings suggested that the naturally being factory composites could shield off inflammation and fat immersion.

17 Stay harmonious

" Leaves, recesses, crazy work weeks, it does not count. Every week, people who remain spare, stick to their healthy habits," Langowski tells us." My most successful guests are the bones who stay harmonious with their exercises throughout the time; they do not let anything get in the way of their drill! It's like putting on their pants or brushing their teeth and is a commodity that they wouldn't be able to do!"

The same intelligence should hold true for your diet, too. The maturity of people who lose weight and keep it off, report that their diet is the same on both the weekends and weekdays, according to an American Journal of Clinical Nutrition report. Simply put, do not go crazy eating bodies, pizza and cheat reflections just because it's Saturday. Your body does not watch what day of the week it is, and neither should you.

18 Limit screen time

Curious what differently successful disasters do? Well, we'll tell you one thing they do not do Netflix and bite. The average American watches 28 hours of television per week, while the NWCR reports that those who have exfoliated 30 pounds and kept it off for at least a time, log smaller than 10 hours per week in front of the blunder tube.

19 Follow the plate rule

Counting calories may have helped you lose weight originally, but as you might have guessed, it's not a habit you can maintain for life. rather, hold onto your flat belly and lose weight permanently with the help of the plate rule." I noway recommend counting calories to any of my guests," says Smith." rather, I tell them to fill 50% of their plate at each mess with non-starchy vegetables like kale, broccoli and carrots. This ensures that they'll take in a fair quantum of fiber, which promotes malnutrition and weight conservation."

Unrefined carbohydrates like sap, sweet potatoes and whole grains should make up a fourth of the plate and the last fourth should be reserved for spare proteins. exploration backs Smith's claim A Brigham Young University College study set up that women who consume further fiber have a significantly lower threat of gaining weight than those who eat lower of the nutrient, likely because they consumed smaller overall calories throughout the day.

20 Do not get discouraged

Last, and most importantly do not get discouraged if the scale swings overhead a bit. recesses, leaves, and stressful life situations be, and not to mention, weight oscillations are completely normal.However, take it with a grain of swab but do not forget about it, If you feel your pants getting tighter. Examine what you are doing else and commit to getting back on the crusade it's as simple as that! And always flash back , conservation is a marathon, not a sprint; you are in this for life! To set yourself for indeed further success, you should read up on the 30 effects You Should Absolutely noway Do If You Want to Lose Weight.

www.ingramcontent.com/pod-product-compliance
Lightning Source LLC
LaVergne TN
LVHW050343160826
845677LV00014B/3770
* 9 7 9 8 8 4 8 6 4 6 2 8 3 *